W9-AYR-650

WELCOME TO MY COUNTRY

Welcome to
IRAQ

Gareth Stevens Publishing
A WORLD ALMANAC EDUCATION GROUP COMPANY

Written by
SONALI MALHOTRA

Edited by
MELVIN NEO

Edited in USA by
JENETTE DONOVAN GUNTLY

Designed by
GEOSLYN LIM

Picture research by
SUSAN JANE MANUEL

First published in North America in 2004 by
Gareth Stevens Publishing
A World Almanac Education Group Company
330 West Olive Street, Suite 100
Milwaukee, Wisconsin 53212 USA

Please visit our web site at:
www.garethstevens.com
For a free color catalog describing
Gareth Stevens Publishing's list of high-quality
books and multimedia programs,
call 1-800-542-2595 (USA) or
1-800-387-3178 (Canada).
Gareth Stevens Publishing's fax: (414) 332-3567.

© **TIMES MEDIA PRIVATE LIMITED** 2004
Originated and designed by
Times Editions
An imprint of Times Media Private Limited
A member of the Times Publishing Group
Times Centre, 1 New Industrial Road
Singapore 536196
http://www.timesone.com.sg/te

Library of Congress Cataloging-in-Publication Data
available upon request from publisher.
Fax (414) 336-0157 for the attention of the
Publishing Records Department.

ISBN 0-8368-2559-4 (lib. bdg.)

Printed in Singapore

1 2 3 4 5 6 7 8 9 08 07 06 05 04

PICTURE CREDITS
Agence France Presse: 3 (bottom), 22,
    38 (bottom)
Art Directors & TRIP Photo Library: 5, 7,
    15 (top), 17, 18 (bottom), 24, 29, 33,
    44 (both)
Tor Eigeland: 37
Getty Images/Hulton Archive: 15 (bottom),
    38 (top)
Haga Library, Japan: 4, 6, 32, 34
HBL Photo Network Agency: 3 (top),14,
    16 (top), 23
Hutchison Library: cover, 1, 20
Klingwalls Geografiska Fárgfotos: 8, 12,
    13, 16 (bottom), 30, 31, 41
North Wind Picture Archive: 2, 11
Christine Osborne Pictures: 18 (top), 19
Jaime Simson: 3 (middle), 21, 26
Nik Wheeler: 9, 10, 25, 27, 28, 35, 36,
    39, 40, 43, 45

Digital Scanning by Superskill Graphics Pte Ltd

Contents

Words that appear in the glossary are printed in **boldface** type the first time they occur in the text.

Welcome to Iraq!

The Republic of Iraq has a very rich and colorful history dating back to 120,000 B.C. Located in the Middle East, the country has ancient rivers, vast deserts, and rugged mountains. Iraq became independent in 1932. From 1968 to 2003, Iraq was under the rule of a **dictator**. Let's learn more about this ancient land and its people.

Opposite: Babylon is an ancient city in Iraq. Many of the groups that ruled the country used Babylon as their capital city.

Below: This Kurdish man is selling vegetables at a stand. The Kurds are an **ethnic** group that lives in northern Iraq.

The Flag of Iraq

The flag of Iraq has three horizontal stripes — red, white, and black. There are three green stars against the white middle stripe. Written in between the stars are the words *"Allahu Akbar"* (ah-LAH-who AHK-bar), which means "God is great."

The Land

Iraq has an area of 168,710 square miles (437,072 square kilometers). Its neighbors are Saudi Arabia, Turkey, Iran, Kuwait, Jordan, and Syria. In the southeast of Iraq lies 36 miles (58 km) of the Persian Gulf coastline. Iraq's two main rivers are the Euphrates and the Tigris. The rivers offer Iraqis water for crops, for drinking, and for travel.

Below: Baghdad, Iraq's capital and its largest city, is located on the banks of the Tigris River. The city's location has played an important role in the history of Iraq.

Rugged mountains cover much of Iraq's northern and eastern areas. The country's highest peak, Haji Ibrahim, is 11,812 feet (3,600 meters) tall and lies near the country's northern border with Iran. To the west of the mountains, the land is good for farming. Large plains cover a large area of central Iraq. The south and southwest of the country are covered in desert regions. The dry land is so harsh that few people live there.

Above: Iraq has mountains in the north and deserts in the south. In between are lush, green valleys.

Climate

Iraq has a dry season and a wet season. The country's dry season is from May to October. Iraq's wet season is from November to April. During the wet season, the country can get almost 40 inches (102 centimeters) of rain.

In summer, temperatures can reach up to 123° Fahrenheit (51° Celsius). Winter temperatures in Iraq are mild and do not often go below freezing, except in the northern mountains.

Below: The farming areas surrounding the city of Mosul have good weather all year. Summers are very mild and winters are warm.

Plants and Animals

Many kinds of plants grow in Iraq, from junipers and wild pears in the mountains to willows and **licorice** along the Tigris and Euphrates rivers. Plantain grows in the plains and date palms grow all over the country.

A variety of animals live in Iraq, including mountain goats, deer, wild pigs, foxes, and wildcats. Partridges, vultures, and hawks are just a few of the birds that live in the country.

Above: Camels can live without food and water for many days, which makes them useful for traveling across the deserts of Iraq. Camels are known as "ships of the desert" because of the way they seem to float across the sand while walking.

History

Between 3500 and 2400 B.C., the Sumerians lived in what is now Iraq. At that time, the country was called Mesopotamia, or "the land between two rivers," because it was located between the Tigris and the Euphrates rivers. The Sumerians invented the wheel, the calendar, the plow, and writing. In 2340 B.C., the Sumerians lost their **empire** to the Akkadians, who then ruled for two hundred years.

Below:
The Sumerians knew a lot about creating strong buildings and temples. Many of the buildings that the Sumerians created, such as this one in the ancient city of Babylon, are still standing today.

Left: The Code of Hammurabi gave Babylonians a strict set of rules about marriage, business, property, and slavery. The code was carved into a tall, black stone pillar called a stele, which was placed in public for all to see and obey.

After the Akkadians lost power, many different groups ruled the country. In 1792 B.C., King Hammurabi took over. He named his new empire Babylonia and made Babylon the capital city. The empire lost power after the king's death and was split into two parts — Babylon and Assyria. By 539 B.C., Babylon had been taken over by invaders from what is now Iran. In 320 B.C., Alexander the Great took over Babylon and Assyria.

Invasions and Empires

In the eighth century A.D., a group of Arabs called the Abbasids invaded Iraq. Baghdad became their capital city. Many people came to Baghdad to study medicine, mathematics, and the arts. In 1258, the Mongols from central Asia **conquered** Iraq. Later, the Ottoman Turks began to take over the country. In 1534, they took control of Baghdad. The Ottoman Empire ruled Iraq until 1917.

Below: The Abbasids valued the arts and learning. During their rule, they built beautiful buildings and fountains like these. The rule of the Abbasids is called the "golden age" of culture and the arts in Iraq.

Modern Times

From 1920 to 1932, Britain ruled Iraq. After Iraq gained its independence, it became a **monarchy**. In 1958, an Iraqi military group killed the prime minister and king. The group then took over and made Iraq a **republic**. Other groups later fought for control until, in 1979, Saddam Hussein became president. He ruled as a dictator until 2003.

Above: The Freedom Monument is located at Al-Tahrir Square in Baghdad. It was built in honor of the 1958 **uprising** in Iraq.

Iraq at War

In 1980, under Saddam Hussein, Iraq invaded Iran. The war ended in 1988. In 1990, Iraq invaded Kuwait. A group of nations, led by the United States, forced the Iraqis out of Kuwait in the Persian Gulf War. In 2003, the U.S. and Britain went to war with Iraq again and removed Saddam Hussein from power. They believed Iraq was making weapons that could kill millions of people. Since then, Iraq has struggled to become a free and stable country.

Left: After the Persian Gulf War, the United Nations (U.N.) made rules about the weapons Iraq could have. Experts, such as these inspectors, were sent to watch over the country's weapons factories. For over ten years, however, Saddam Hussein would not let them into some places, which led to the 2003 attack on the country by the United States and Britain.

Nebuchadnezzar II
(c.630 B.C.–562 B.C.)

Nebuchadnezzar ruled Babylon, one of the two kingdoms formed when the old Babylonian Empire fell apart. The king was very interested in architecture and had many great structures built, such as the Ishtar Gate and the famous Hanging Gardens of Babylon.

King Faisal I

King Faisal I (1885–1933)

In 1921, the British selected Faisal I to become king of Iraq. A vote by the Iraqi people made it official. During his rule, Faisal helped the country become independent. He also helped Iraq join the League of Nations.

Nuri es-Said

Nuri es-Said (1888–1958)

As prime minister from 1953 to 1958, Nuri es-Said helped Iraq become more modern and to trade with other nations. He was killed in 1958 when a military group took over the country.

Government and the Economy

From 1968 to 2003, the Ba'ath Party was the only political party in Iraq. It was led by Saddam Hussein, who also served as president and prime minister of the country.

Iraq's national assembly has 250 members. Assembly members represent Iraq's eighteen **provinces**, and each member serves a four-year term.

Above: In 1979, when he first came to power, Saddam Hussein had the support of nations around the world. Because of crimes against his own people, especially the Kurds, he is now believed to have been one of the most dangerous dictators on Earth.

Left: Before the war in 2003, paintings and statues of Saddam Hussein could be found all over Iraq. Most are now gone.

Left: In order to take part in Iraqi government, the Kurds formed the Kurdish Legislative Council, with the permission of Saddam Hussein. Under Hussein's rules, Kurds were not allowed to serve in Iraq's national assembly.

The Court System

Iraq's court system has three levels. The country's highest court is the Court of Cassation. Iraq's religious courts hear cases about religion, marriage, and **inheritance**. Special courts hear cases about national security.

The Presidency

According to Iraq's **constitution**, the person who serves as the head of the country's Revolutionary Command Council (RCC) also becomes president of Iraq. From 1979 to 2003, Saddam Hussein filled both positions.

Economy

Most of Iraq's money comes from oil. After the 1990 Persian Gulf War, the U.N. made rules about how much oil Iraq could sell to other nations. The rules were made so that Iraq would not have enough money to build more weapons. Starting in 1997, Iraq was allowed to **export** enough oil to pay for medical supplies and food.

Above: Tank trucks like this one move oil across Iraq. In the Persian Gulf War, many of Iraq's oil plants and trucks were destroyed.

Left: These oil pipelines run through Iraq's Kurdish region. Before the Persian Gulf War, Iraq was the second-largest producer of oil in the world. After the war ended, Saddam Hussein refused to allow the U.N. to inspect the nation's weapons. Because of this, Iraq was not allowed to sell most of its oil, and many pipelines have sat unused. Today, it is hoped that selling Iraq's oil will help the country recover from years of war and poverty.

Besides oil, Iraq also produces natural gas, salt, and **phosphates**. The country mines sulfur, too, which is often used in making paper. Although Iraq makes some money from these resources, it is not enough to help the poor economy.

At the time of the war in 2003, Iraq also produced electricity, fuel, cloth, materials for building, chemicals, and food products.

Above: The future of this date farm, located along the Shatt Al-Arab Waterway in Basra, may be uncertain after the 2003 war. Dates and other fruits, including grapes and melons, have long been an important part of the country's farming industry.

People and Lifestyle

Most Iraqis are Arabs who belong to the religion of Islam. Some Christians and Jews also live in Iraq. Many Iraqis live in cities, where they can find jobs.

Ethnic Groups

After Arabs, Kurds are Iraq's second largest ethnic group. They live in the mountains in northeastern Iraq.

Below: The Kurds lead a simple life. Most Kurds work as shepherds or farmers. In recent times, however, many Kurds have moved to cities in search of jobs.

The *Ma'dan* (MAH-dan), or Marsh Arabs, live in the marshes between the Euphrates and Tigris rivers. To live, the Ma'dan fish and hunt.

The Bedouin are **nomads** and often live in tents made of goat or camel hair. They follow their herds of sheep and goats as they roam through the desert.

Other ethnic groups in Iraq include the Turkomans, the *Yazidis* (yah-ZEE-deez), and the Sabeans.

Above:
The Ma'dan, who live in the marshes of southern Iraq, build their houses out of reeds. The homes have no running water or electricity and are lifted above the ground to keep them dry.

Family Life

Iraqi families are usually large, and family relationships are close. Most families live in one house, which is expanded when the family grows. Children often live with their parents until they are twenty-five years old.

Most Iraqi marriages are arranged by the couple's parents. The groom signs a contract to make the marriage official.

Below: A group of Yazidi women have gathered in Mosul to pray. Yazidis are a very close group. They do not mix with other people, and Yazidi men and women never marry anyone from outside of their ethnic group.

Women in Iraq

In the past, Iraqi women married young and had a family. In the 1920s, many women began to enter the **workforce**.

After the Persian Gulf War, the bad economy forced many women to lose their jobs. Hussein's government then created laws against women working. Now, Iraqi women are fighting to hold onto their other rights, such as voting.

Above:
Unlike some other Islamic countries in the Middle East, the women in Iraq are not required to wear an *abbayah* (ah-BYE-ah), a long gown with a veil that covers most of a woman's face. Muslim women in Iraq often do wear a *hijab* (hih-JOB), which is a head scarf that does not cover their faces.

Education

In Iraq, education is considered very important. In 1850, only 1 percent of all Iraqis were able to read and write. Today, this number has risen to more than 58 percent. Schooling is free for Iraqi children, and they must attend classes from age six to age eleven.

Iraq is one of the few Arab countries that encourages girls to receive an education. In addition, both men and women can serve as teachers in Iraq.

Below: All children in Iraq, including these students in Baghdad, must attend classes. Even the smallest Iraqi villages have their own schools.

About half of all Iraqi students go on to secondary school, which lasts six years. In their third year, students can choose to take **vocational** classes.

Iraq has eight universities. Four are located in Baghdad. The others are in Arbil, Mosul, Al Basrah, and Tikrit. Iraq also has institutions that teach subjects such as farming and **technology**.

Above: In Iraq, children often take classes outside of school, such as this art class being held in Baghdad.

25

Religion

About 97 percent of Iraq's population follows the Islamic religion. Followers of Islam, who are called Muslims, must live by a set of religious rules called the Five Pillars of Islam. The rules include reciting, "There is no God but Allah, and Muhammad is His messenger," praying five times a day, giving money to the poor, fasting during the Islamic holy month, and making at least one **pilgrimage** to Mecca, in Saudi Arabia.

Below: This gold-domed **mosque**, called the Mosque of Iman Ali, is one example of Islamic architecture. Since the Islamic religion came to Iraq in the seventh century, Muslims have been building majestic mosques all across the country.

Muslims in Iraq are divided into two groups: the Shi'ites and the Sunnis. The Shi'ites believe that only relatives of the prophet Muhammad can serve as religious leaders. The Sunnis believe that anyone educated in the Islamic religion can lead.

Of the small number of Iraqis who are non-Muslim, Christians make up the largest group. Most Christian Iraqis are Roman Catholic.

Above: In Iraq, Christians must go to churches, such as the Church of Tahira in the city of Qaraqosh, to pray. The country forbids Christians to talk about their faith or hold any religious event outside of their church.

Language

Iraq's official language is Arabic, which is read from right to left. The language's twenty-eight letters are written differently depending on where they fall: at the beginning, middle, or end of a word. Arabic is a hard language to speak because many of the sounds are made deep in the throat and are hard to learn.

Left: Because most Iraqis can read, bookstands such as this one in Baghdad are very popular.

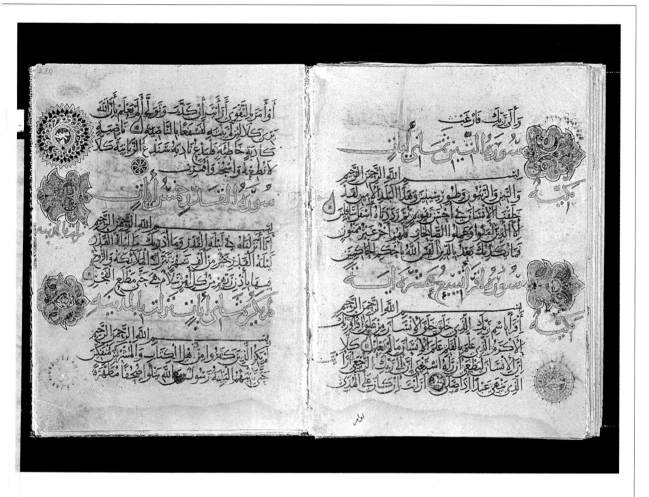

Literature

Because some of the world's earliest examples of writing have been found in Iraq, experts believe written language may have started in that land.

Iraq has produced many authors and poets, including Rabi'a al-Adawiyya, who lived during the 700s; Muhammad Mahdi al-Jawahiri (1900–1997); and Nazik al-Mala'ika (1922–).

Above: Antique copies of the Koran, the Islamic holy book, can be found in many museums in Iraq. The books were handwritten in Arabic, which is full of graceful loops and swirls.

29

Arts

Iraq has a rich tradition in architecture, pottery, painting, music, and weaving. Iraqi art is largely influenced by Islam, which does not allow artists to show images of people. Most artwork in Iraq is done in **arabesque**, which uses lots of flower shapes, circles, and squares.

The people of Iraq value art. Often, the country's museums pay local artists to create artworks they can exhibit.

Below: This artist has a shop in the city of Baghdad, where he sells his modern paintings. Many Iraqis enjoy the arts, including music, painting, and sculpture.

In Iraq, writing the Arabic language in **calligraphy** is a popular art form. It is often used to decorate buildings and mosques, but may also decorate tiles, plates, or sculptures. Most messages in calligraphy come from the Koran.

Many of the country's monuments and buildings have artistic styles, too. During the rule of Saddam Hussein, architects were ordered only to create buildings in acceptable Iraqi styles.

Above: Architecture in Baghdad is a mix of the old and new. Ancient monuments stand next to new, modern buildings, which creates an interesting blend of styles.

Dance

Folk dancing is a popular form of entertainment in Iraq. Each region of the country has its own folk dances. During the Kurdish New Year and at weddings, the Kurds perform a dance while standing in a circle. The Bedouin have their own dance, the Hagallah, which is danced in a line. The Hagallah is performed during the date harvest.

Below: Many folk dances in Iraq are designed to help men and women find future wives and husbands. To draw attention, the dancers often wear colorful costumes.

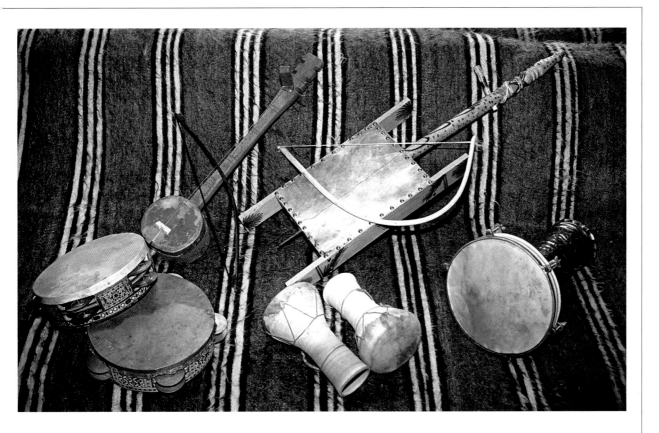

Music

Traditional Iraqi music is very lively. The performers often **chant**, clap their hands, or play drums. Iraq has several traditional instruments, including the *oud* (OOD), which is shaped like a guitar. The *riqq* (REEK), a kind of tambourine, usually keeps the beat alongside other traditional instruments. Bedouin musicians often play the *rebaba* (rah-BAH-bah), a one-stringed, fiddle-like instrument.

Above: The oud, rebaba, and riqq, along with various hand drums, are instruments used to play traditional Iraqi music.

Leisure

Most Iraqis work a six-day week that lasts from Saturday through Thursday. They only take off on Friday, which is the Muslim holy day. Iraqis spend most of their free time with family members and close friends. They go on outings or visit each other at home. Since the Persian Gulf War, people in Iraq have had less money for leisure activities. They spend much more time at home.

Below: Islam does not encourage men and women to mix with one another. Women only go out with female friends or family members.

In their free time, Iraqis like to watch movies and television, read, and listen to music. Chess and backgammon are popular board games. Iraqi men meet at cafés during lunch breaks and after work. There, they talk with friends and read newspapers. Women visit friends, and children play sports and take dance and music classes. Since the war, there are fewer celebrations and festivals.

Above: During their long lunch breaks, some Iraqi men like to play backgammon.

Sports

Iraq's most popular game is soccer. Soccer is played in schoolyards and parks across the country. Almost every neighborhood has its own soccer team.

In Iraq, women also play sports. In the Muslim Women's Games, which are for female athletes from Islamic countries, women compete in events such as gymnastics and swimming.

Below: Because sports are so popular in Iraq, the government often holds large competitions. This colorful display in Baghdad's national stadium marks the start of the Annual Police Games.

Left: The Bedouin enjoy hunting with **falcons**, which are good at catching rabbits, **jerboas**, and other animals. This Bedouin man wears a thick glove to protect his hand and arm from the bird's sharp claws.

Some Iraqis also enjoy sports such as basketball and volleyball. Popular individual sports include weight lifting and boxing. Many Iraqis like to attend sporting events in person, but the larger events are broadcast on television, too.

Holidays

Iraq observes both official holidays and religious holidays. During the official holidays, all public offices, businesses, and schools are closed. These holidays are New Year's Day (January 1), Army Day (January 6), Revolution Anniversary Day (February 8), FAO Day (April 17), Labor Day (May 1), National Day (July 14), Ba'ath Revolution Day (July 17), and Peace Day (August 8).

Above: Muslim women recite prayers during the Eid al-Fitr festival.

Below: Before 2003, the Ba'ath Party held Revolution Anniversary Day parades.

Religious Festivals

Eid al-Fitr (EED AHL-fitr) is a three-day festival at the end of the Muslim holy month of Ramadan. *Eid al-Adha* (EED AHL-ad-ha) celebrates Muslims' *hajj* (HAAJ), or pilgrimage, to the holy city of Mecca, in Saudi Arabia. Iraqis also honor the prophet Muhammad's birthday. The Shi'ite holiday *Ashura* (as-SHOO-rah) remembers the religious **martyr** Imam Hussein.

Above: Iraqi girls march in a street parade to mark the arrival of spring. In addition to such local festivals, Iraq hosts gatherings of artists, writers, and poets from all over the world.

Food

Iraqi cuisine is rich and varied. Their dishes do not contain pork or alcohol because Islam forbids these two items. Iraqis enjoy rice, yogurt, pita bread, and kabobs, which are chunks of meat grilled on sticks. One Iraqi specialty, *masgouf* (MAAS-goof), is made of fish. Other popular dishes are *quzi* (KOO-zee), or stuffed roasted lamb; and *kibba* (kih-BAH), or fried meatballs.

Left: Masgouf is a traditional Iraqi dish of grilled fish with sliced onions and tomatoes. The dish is often served with bread.

All meals are generally eaten with *samoons* (SAH-moons), or traditional bread. Iraqis also have a fondness for sweets. Their desert specialties include *baklava* (baa-KLAH-vah), a pastry filled with honey and nuts; *murabba amar* (moor-ah-bah AH-mar), dates in syrup; *zlabiya* (zlah-BEE-yah), date pastries; and fresh fruits. To finish off the meal, Iraqis often drink Arabic coffee or sweet tea after dinner.

Above: Lavish meals such as this one were more common before the Persian Gulf War. Since the war and the collapse of the economy, however, food has become scarce and very expensive in Iraq.

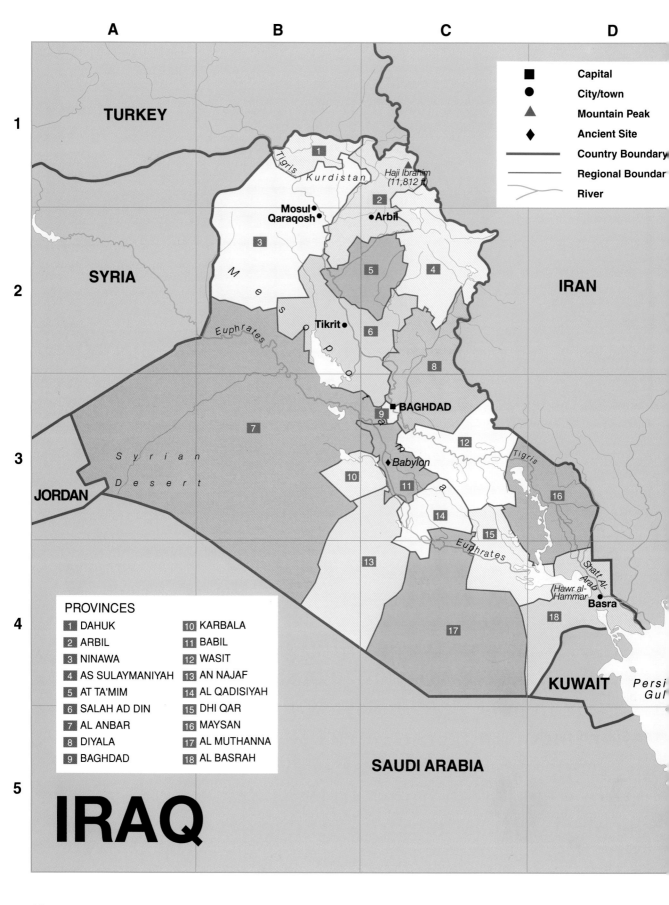

A **B** **C** **D**

1

TURKEY

Tigris

Kurdistan

1

*Haji Ibrahim
(11,812 ft)*

2

Mosul ●
Qaraqosh ●

● **Arbil**

3

M

e

s

5

4

2

SYRIA

IRAN

6

Tikrit ●

Euphrates

o

8

p

■ BAGHDAD

9

12

3

7

S y r i a n

t

a

Tigris

Babylon

D e s e r t

10

11

16

JORDAN

14

15

17

13

Euphrates

Shatt Al-Arab

18

Hawr al-Hammar

Basra

4

KUWAIT

*Persi
Gul*

Legend	
■	Capital
●	City/town
▲	Mountain Peak
◆	Ancient Site
——	Country Boundary
——	Regional Boundar
〜〜	River

PROVINCES

1	DAHUK	10	KARBALA
2	ARBIL	11	BABIL
3	NINAWA	12	WASIT
4	AS SULAYMANIYAH	13	AN NAJAF
5	AT TA'MIM	14	AL QADISIYAH
6	SALAH AD DIN	15	DHI QAR
7	AL ANBAR	16	MAYSAN
8	DIYALA	17	AL MUTHANNA
9	BAGHDAD	18	AL BASRAH

SAUDI ARABIA

5

IRAQ

Above: The Ma'dan build their homes using reeds, which are found along the riverbanks.

Al Anbar (province)
A2–C3
Al Basrah
(province)
C4–D4
Al Muthanna
(province) C3–C4
Al Qadisiyah
(province) C3–C4
An Najaf (province)
B3–C4
Arbil (city) C2
Arbil (province)
B1–C2
As Sulaymaniyah
(province) C1–C2
At Ta'mim (province)
B2–C2

Babil (province) C3
Babylon C3
Baghdad (city) C3

Baghdad
(province) C3
Basra D4

Dahuk (province) B1
Dhi Qar (province)
C3–D4
Diyala (province)
C2–C3

Euphrates River
B2–C4

Haji Ibrahim C1
Hawr al-Hammar
C4–D4

Iran C1–D4

Jordan A3

Karbala (province)
B3–C3
Kurdistan B1–B2
Kuwait D4–D5

Maysan (province)
C3–D4
Mesopotamia B2–C3
Mosul B1

Ninawa (province)
B1–B2

Persian Gulf D4–D5

Qaraqosh B2

Salah ad Din
(province) B2–C3

Saudi Arabia A3–D5
Shatt Al-Arab
Waterway D4
Syria A1–B2
Syrian Desert
A3–B3

Tigris River B1–D4
Tikrit B2
Turkey A1–C1

Wasit (province) C3

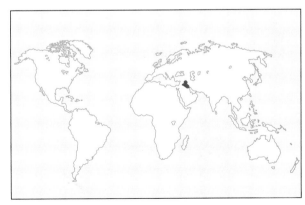

Quick Facts

Official Name   Republic of Iraq

Capital   Baghdad

Official Language   Arabic

Population   23,331,985 (July 2001)

Land Area   168,710 square miles (437,072 sq km)

Provinces   Al Anbar, Al Basrah, Al Muthanna, Al Qadisiyah, An Najaf, Arbil, As Sulaymaniyah, At Ta'mim, Babil, Baghdad, Dahuk, Dhi Qar, Diyala, Karbala, Maysan, Ninawa, Salah ad Din, Wasit

Highest Point   Haji Ibrahim 11,812 feet (3,600 meters)

Major Rivers   Euphrates, Tigris

Major Lake   Hawr al-Hammar

Main Religion   Islam

Major Holidays   New Year's Day (January 1), Army Day (January 6), Revolution Anniversary (February 8), FAO Day (April 17), Labor Day (May 1), National Day (July 14), Ba'ath Revolution Day (July 17), Peace Day (August 8)

National Anthem   Land of Two Rivers

Currency   Iraqi dinar (0.31 dinar = U.S.$1 in 2003)

Opposite: Camels are one of the few animals that can survive in the heat of Iraq's deserts.

Glossary

arabesque: a style of art that uses the outlines of geometric shapes, fruits, or flowers to make a pattern.

calligraphy: handwriting done in a very artistic, graceful style.

chant: to sing or repeat a sound or words over and over again.

conquered: invaded and took over a land using force.

constitution: a set of laws that say how a country's government should be run and what rights citizens have.

dictator: a ruler who has complete control over a country.

empire: a very large collection of lands or regions ruled by one group.

ethnic: related to a certain race or culture of people who have similar customs and languages.

export (v): to sell and ship products to other countries.

falcons: a kind of hawk that people can train to hunt.

inheritance: the act of receiving money, valuable objects, or land after a family member has died.

jerboas: small, jumping rodents with long back legs and tails.

licorice: a plant that is often used to make candy.

martyr: a person who believes strongly enough in a religion that he or she accepts death rather than give it up.

monarchy: a system of government controlled by a king or a queen.

mosque: a place of worship for Muslims.

nomads: people who move from place to place and who often live in tents.

phosphates: acids that, when broken down, can be used to make bubbly drinks or be used in fertilizer.

pilgrimage: a journey made to a holy place as an act of religious devotion.

provinces: regions of a country that are given fixed borders and their own local government officials.

republic: a country in which citizens elect their own lawmakers.

technology: using machines to do jobs.

uprising: an act of violence by citizens to fight against a government's rules.

vocational: relating to a job, profession, or skilled trade.

workforce: the people in a country who work, most often outside the home.

More Books to Read

Ancient Mesopotamia. Let's See Library Ancient Civilizations series. Robert B. Noyed and Cynthia Fitterer Klingel (Compass Point Books)

The City of Rainbows: A Tale from Ancient Sumer. Karen Sharp Foster (Univ Museum Pubns)

Daily Life in Ancient and Modern Baghdad. Cities through time series. Dawn Kotapish (Lerner)

Iraq: A country in conflict. The Here and Now Reproducible Book series. Carole Marsh (Gallopade Publication Group)

Iraq. Countries series. Tamara L. Britton (Checkerboard Library)

Mesopotamia. Cultures of the Past series. Pamela F. Service (Marshall Cavendish Corporation)

Mesopotamia. Ancient Civilization series. Tami Deedrick (Raintree Steck-Vaughn)

Saddam Hussein (Major World Leaders) Charles J. Shields (Chelsea House Publishing)

The Sumerians. Understanding People in the Past series. Naida Kirkpatrick (Heinemann Library)

The Tigris and Euphrates Rivers. Watts Library series. Melissa Whitcraft (Franklin Watts)

Videos

Ancient Mesopotamia. (Schlessinger)

The Middle East. (Schlessinger)

U.S. Politics 1980–2000. (Schlessinger)

Web Sites

news.bbc.co.uk/cbbcnews/hi/find_out/ guides/world/iraq/newsid_2181000/ 2181236.stm

teacher.scholastic.com/scholasticnews/ indepth/war-iraq/

www.timeforkids.com/TFK/specials/ iraq/0,8805,424876,00.html

www.worldalmanacforkids.com/ explore/nations/iraq.html

Due to the dynamic nature of the Internet, some web sites stay current longer than others. To find additional web sites, use a reliable search engine with one or more of the following keywords to help you locate information about Iraq. Keywords: *Baghdad, calligraphy, Mesopotamia, oil, Persian Gulf War, Saddam Hussein.*

Index